The Book Lover's Book Journal

SL Beaumont

ISBN: 978-1790273546

Independently published by:
Paperback Writer's Publishing
Auckland, New Zealand

This Book Journal Belongs To:

. . . .

Contents

SL BEAUMONT

Introduction

If like me, you enjoy books and reading, then you'll love this handy Book Lover's Book Journal. It's a place to note down your all-important 'To Read List', details of your most-loved books, set yourself reading challenges and a place to review books as you read them.

Whether you read print books, ebooks, listen to audiobooks or a mixture, then this journal is a great place to record your reading experiences, likes and dislikes.

Do you need somewhere to keep the details of that great book you would like to recommend to a friend? Do you want to expand the genre of books that you read? Or do you need to quickly find the details of the next book on your reading list? Then this journal is for you.

I've also included several blank 'Ideas' pages at the back so that all of you budding novelists can make note of those fabulous ideas when inspiration hits!

Enjoy!

"A room without books is like a body without a soul."
-Marcus Tillius Cicero

My To Read List

Title	Author

"Beware of the person of one book."
-Thomas Aquinas

My To Read List

Title	Author

"To learn to read is to light a fire; every syllable that is spelled out is a spark."
-Victor Hugo

My Top Books of All Time

	Title	Author
1		
2		
3		
4		
5		
6		
7		
8		
9		
10		
11		
12		
13		
14		
15		

Reading Challenges

Reading Challenges are a great way to break out of a rut or to supplement your reading. The following challenges have been designed as one book per month. Try one or design your own on page 21.

Reading Challenge #1

1. Read a classic

2. Read a Young Adult novel

3. Read a poetry collection or anthology

4. Read a biography or autobiography

5. Read a sci-fi novel

6. Read a non-fiction work

7. Read a graphic novel

8. Read a paranormal or fantasy novel

9. Read a Scandinavian crime novel

10. Read historical fiction

11. Read a comedy novel or memoir

12. Read a book by an indie author

More Reading Challenges

Reading Challenge #2:

1. Read a Pulitzer or Man Booker Prize winning novel

2. Read a self-improvement book

3. Read a book that has been banned at some point

4. Read a zombie novel

5. Read the first book in a new series

6. Read a book of essays or short stories

7. Read a dystopian or post-apocalyptic novel

8. Read a book that's becoming a movie this year

9. Re-read your best childhood book

10. Read a book translated into English

11. Read a horror novel

12. Read a book set in a culture you're not familiar with

More Reading Challenges

<u>Other Reading Challenges:</u>

1. Read the World Challenge #1
   (read 12 books set in 12 different
   countries)

2. Read the World Challenge #2
   (read 12 books written by authors of 12
   different nationalities)

3. A Series Challenge
   (choose a complete series to read)

4. A Genre Challenge
   (read 12 books from four genres that you
   don't normally read)

5. Classics Challenge
   (read 12 classic novels)

6. Biography Challenge
   (read 12 biographies, autobiographies or
   memoirs)

As you can see, the possibilities are endless.
Turn over to design your own.

More Reading Challenges

Design your own reading challenge:

	Genre, title or type of book
1	
2	
3	
4	
5	
6	
7	
8	
9	
10	
11	
12	

My Partially Read (but really must finish) List

Title	Author	Page

"Choose an author as you choose a friend."
-Sir Christopher Wren

My Much-loved Authors

Author: ....

Titles:

....

....

Author: ....

Titles:

....

....

Author: ....

Titles:

....

....

Author: ....

Titles:

....

....

Memorable Quotes

Quote:

....

....

....

Author: ....

Quote:

....

....

....

Author: ....

Quote:

....

....

....

....

Author: ....

Memorable Quotes

Quote:

....

....

....

....

Author: ....

Quote:

....

....

....

....

Author: ....

Quote:

....

....

....

....

Author: ....

Memorable Quotes

Quote:

....

....

....

....

Author: ....

Quote:

....

....

....

....

Author: ....

Quote:

....

....

....

....

Author: ....

My Reviews

Use the next three pages to index your reviews.

#	Title	Date	Page
1			31
2			33
3			35
4			37
5			39
6			41
7			43
8			45
9			47
10			49
11			51
12			53
13			55
14			57
15			59
16			61

My Reviews

#	Title	Date	Page
17			63
18			65
19			67
20			69
21			71
22			73
23			75
24			77
25			79
26			81
27			83
28			85
29			87
30			89
31			91
32			93
33			95

My Reviews

#	Title	Date	Page
34			97
35			99
36			101
37			103
38			105
39			107
40			109
41			111
42			113
43			115
44			117
45			119
46			121
47			123
48			125
49			127
50			129

#1. Title:

Author: ....

Publisher: ....

Fiction: ◯   Non-Fiction: ◯

Genre / Subject: ....

My review:

....
....
....
....
....
....
....
....
....
....
....
....

Star Rating: ☆☆☆☆☆

#2. Title:

Author: ....

Publisher: ....

Fiction: ◯   Non-Fiction: ◯

Genre / Subject: ....

My review:

....
....
....
....
....
....
....
....
....
....
....
....

Star Rating: ☆☆☆☆☆

#3. Title:

Author: ....

Publisher: ....

Fiction: ◯   Non-Fiction: ◯

Genre / Subject: ....

My review:

....
....
....
....
....
....
....
....
....
....
....
....

Star Rating: ☆☆☆☆☆

#4. Title:

Author: ....

Publisher: ....

Fiction: ◯   Non-Fiction: ◯

Genre / Subject: ....

My review:

....
....
....
....
....
....
....
....
....
....
....
....

Star Rating: ☆☆☆☆☆

#5. Title:

Author: ....

Publisher: ....

Fiction: ◯   Non-Fiction: ◯

Genre / Subject: ....

My review:

....
....
....
....
....
....
....
....
....
....
....
....

Star Rating: ☆☆☆☆☆

#6. Title:

Author: ....

Publisher: ....

Fiction: ◯   Non-Fiction: ◯

Genre / Subject: ....

My review:

....
....
....
....
....
....
....
....
....
....
....
....

Star Rating: ☆☆☆☆☆

#7. Title:

Author: ....

Publisher: ....

Fiction: ◯   Non-Fiction: ◯

Genre / Subject: ....

My review:

....
....
....
....
....
....
....
....
....
....
....
....

Star Rating: ☆☆☆☆☆

#8. Title:

Author: ....

Publisher: ....

Fiction: ◯   Non-Fiction: ◯

Genre / Subject: ....

My review:

....
....
....
....
....
....
....
....
....
....
....
....

Star Rating: ☆☆☆☆☆

#9. Title:

Author: ....

Publisher: ....

Fiction: ◯   Non-Fiction: ◯

Genre / Subject: ....

My review:

....
....
....
....
....
....
....
....
....
....
....
....

Star Rating: ☆☆☆☆☆

#10. Title:

Author: ....

Publisher: ....

Fiction: ◯   Non-Fiction: ◯

Genre / Subject: ....

My review:

....
....
....
....
....
....
....
....
....
....
....
....

Star Rating: ☆ ☆ ☆ ☆ ☆

#11. Title:

Author: ....

Publisher: ....

Fiction: ◯　　　　　Non-Fiction: ◯

Genre / Subject: ....

My review:

....
....
....
....
....
....
....
....
....
....
....
....

Star Rating: ☆☆☆☆☆

#12. Title:

Author: ....

Publisher: ....

Fiction: ◯   Non-Fiction: ◯

Genre / Subject: ....

My review:

....
....
....
....
....
....
....
....
....
....
....
....

Star Rating: ☆☆☆☆☆

#13. Title:

Author: ....

Publisher: ....

Fiction: ◯   Non-Fiction: ◯

Genre / Subject: ....

My review:

....
....
....
....
....
....
....
....
....
....
....
....

Star Rating: ☆☆☆☆☆

#14. Title:

Author: ....

Publisher: ....

Fiction: ◯   Non-Fiction: ◯

Genre / Subject: ....

My review:

....
....
....
....
....
....
....
....
....
....
....
....

Star Rating: ☆☆☆☆☆

#15. Title:

Author: ....

Publisher: ....

Fiction: ◯   Non-Fiction: ◯

Genre / Subject: ....

My review:

....
....
....
....
....
....
....
....
....
....
....
....

Star Rating: ☆☆☆☆☆

#16. Title:

Author: ....

Publisher: ....

Fiction: ◯   Non-Fiction: ◯

Genre / Subject: ....

My review:

....
....
....
....
....
....
....
....
....
....
....
....

Star Rating: ☆☆☆☆☆

#17. Title:

Author: ....

Publisher: ....

Fiction: ◯   Non-Fiction: ◯

Genre / Subject: ....

My review:

....
....
....
....
....
....
....
....
....
....
....
....

Star Rating: ☆☆☆☆☆

#18. Title:

Author: ....

Publisher: ....

Fiction: ◯   Non-Fiction: ◯

Genre / Subject: ....

My review:

....
....
....
....
....
....
....
....
....
....
....
....

Star Rating: ☆☆☆☆☆

#19. Title:

Author: ....

Publisher: ....

Fiction: ◯　　　　　　Non-Fiction: ◯

Genre / Subject: ....

My review:

....

....

....

....

....

....

....

....

....

....

....

....

Star Rating: ☆ ☆ ☆ ☆ ☆

#20. Title:

Author: ....

Publisher: ....

Fiction: ◯   Non-Fiction: ◯

Genre / Subject: ....

My review:

....
....
....
....
....
....
....
....
....
....
....
....

Star Rating: ☆☆☆☆☆

#21. Title:

Author: ....

Publisher: ....

Fiction: ◯   Non-Fiction: ◯

Genre / Subject: ....

My review:

....
....
....
....
....
....
....
....
....
....
....
....

Star Rating: ☆☆☆☆☆

#22. Title:

Author: ....

Publisher: ....

Fiction: ◯   Non-Fiction: ◯

Genre / Subject: ....

My review:

....
....
....
....
....
....
....
....
....
....
....
....

Star Rating: ☆☆☆☆☆

#23. Title:

Author: ....

Publisher: ....

Fiction: ◯   Non-Fiction: ◯

Genre / Subject: ....

My review:

....
....
....
....
....
....
....
....
....
....
....
....

Star Rating: ☆☆☆☆☆

#24. Title:

Author: ....

Publisher: ....

Fiction: ◯   Non-Fiction: ◯

Genre / Subject: ....

My review:

....
....
....
....
....
....
....
....
....
....
....
....

Star Rating: ☆☆☆☆☆

#25. Title:

Author: ....

Publisher: ....

Fiction: ◯   Non-Fiction: ◯

Genre / Subject: ....

My review:

....
....
....
....
....
....
....
....
....
....
....
....

Star Rating: ☆ ☆ ☆ ☆ ☆

#26. Title:

Author: ....

Publisher: ....

Fiction: ◯   Non-Fiction: ◯

Genre / Subject: ....

My review:

....
....
....
....
....
....
....
....
....
....
....
....

Star Rating: ☆☆☆☆☆

#27. Title:

Author: ....

Publisher: ....

Fiction: ◯   Non-Fiction: ◯

Genre / Subject: ....

My review:

....
....
....
....
....
....
....
....
....
....
....
....

Star Rating: ☆ ☆ ☆ ☆ ☆

#28. Title:

Author: ....

Publisher: ....

Fiction: ○   Non-Fiction: ○

Genre / Subject: ....

My review:

....
....
....
....
....
....
....
....
....
....
....
....

Star Rating: ☆☆☆☆☆

#29. Title:

Author: ....

Publisher: ....

Fiction: ◯   Non-Fiction: ◯

Genre / Subject: ....

My review:

....
....
....
....
....
....
....
....
....
....
....
....

Star Rating: ☆☆☆☆☆

#30. Title:

Author: ....

Publisher: ....

Fiction: ◯   Non-Fiction: ◯

Genre / Subject: ....

My review:

....
....
....
....
....
....
....
....
....
....
....
....
....

Star Rating: ☆☆☆☆☆

#31. Title:

Author: ....

Publisher: ....

Fiction: ◯   *Non-Fiction:* ◯

Genre / Subject: ....

My review:

....
....
....
....
....
....
....
....
....
....
....
....

Star Rating: ☆☆☆☆☆

#32. Title:

Author: ....

Publisher: ....

Fiction: ◯   Non-Fiction: ◯

Genre / Subject: ....

My review:

....
....
....
....
....
....
....
....
....
....
....
....
....

Star Rating: ☆☆☆☆☆

#33. Title:

Author: ....

Publisher: ....

Fiction: ◯   Non-Fiction: ◯

Genre / Subject: ....

My review:

....
....
....
....
....
....
....
....
....
....
....
....
....

Star Rating: ☆☆☆☆☆

#34. Title:

Author: ....

Publisher: ....

Fiction: ◯   Non-Fiction: ◯

Genre / Subject: ....

My review:

....
....
....
....
....
....
....
....
....
....
....
....

Star Rating: ☆☆☆☆☆

#35. Title:

Author: ....

Publisher: ....

Fiction: ◯   Non-Fiction: ◯

Genre / Subject: ....

My review:

....
....
....
....
....
....
....
....
....
....
....
....
....

Star Rating: ☆☆☆☆☆

#36. Title:

Author: ....

Publisher: ....

Fiction: ◯   Non-Fiction: ◯

Genre / Subject: ....

My review:

....
....
....
....
....
....
....
....
....
....
....
....

Star Rating: ☆☆☆☆☆

#37. Title:

Author: ....

Publisher: ....

Fiction: ◯   Non-Fiction: ◯

Genre / Subject: ....

My review:

....
....
....
....
....
....
....
....
....
....
....
....

Star Rating: ☆☆☆☆☆

#38. Title:

Author: ....

Publisher: ....

Fiction: ◯   Non-Fiction: ◯

Genre / Subject: ....

My review:

....
....
....
....
....
....
....
....
....
....
....
....

Star Rating: ☆☆☆☆☆

#39. Title:

Author: ....

Publisher: ....

Fiction: ○   Non-Fiction: ○

Genre / Subject: ....

My review:

....
....
....
....
....
....
....
....
....
....
....
....

Star Rating: ☆☆☆☆☆

#40. Title:

Author: ....

Publisher: ....

Fiction: ◯   Non-Fiction: ◯

Genre / Subject: ....

My review:

....
....
....
....
....
....
....
....
....
....
....
....
....

Star Rating: ☆☆☆☆☆

#41. Title:

Author: ....

Publisher: ....

Fiction: ◯   Non-Fiction: ◯

Genre / Subject: ....

My review:

....
....
....
....
....
....
....
....
....
....
....
....

Star Rating: ☆☆☆☆☆

#42. Title:

Author: ....

Publisher: ....

Fiction: ◯   Non-Fiction: ◯

Genre / Subject: ....

My review:

....
....
....
....
....
....
....
....
....
....
....
....
....

Star Rating: ☆☆☆☆☆

#43. Title:

Author: ....

Publisher: ....

Fiction: ◯   Non-Fiction: ◯

Genre / Subject: ....

My review:

....
....
....
....
....
....
....
....
....
....
....
....

Star Rating: ☆ ☆ ☆ ☆ ☆

#44. Title:

Author: ....

Publisher: ....

Fiction: ⭘   Non-Fiction: ⭘

Genre / Subject: ....

My review:

....
....
....
....
....
....
....
....
....
....
....
....

Star Rating: ☆☆☆☆☆

#45. Title:

Author: ....

Publisher: ....

Fiction: ○   Non-Fiction: ○

Genre / Subject: ....

My review:

....
....
....
....
....
....
....
....
....
....
....

Star Rating: ☆☆☆☆☆

#46. Title:

Author: ....

Publisher: ....

Fiction: ◯   Non-Fiction: ◯

Genre / Subject: ....

My review:

....
....
....
....
....
....
....
....
....
....
....
....
....

Star Rating: ☆☆☆☆☆

#47. Title:

Author: ....

Publisher: ....

Fiction: ◯   Non-Fiction: ◯

Genre / Subject: ....

My review:
....
....
....
....
....
....
....
....
....
....
....
....
....
....

Star Rating: ☆☆☆☆☆

#48. Title:

Author: ....

Publisher: ....

Fiction: ◯   Non-Fiction: ◯

Genre / Subject: ....

My review:

....
....
....
....
....
....
....
....
....
....
....
....
....

Star Rating: ☆☆☆☆☆

#49. Title:

Author: ....

Publisher: ....

Fiction: ◯   Non-Fiction: ◯

Genre / Subject: ....

My review:

....
....
....
....
....
....
....
....
....
....
....
....
....

Star Rating: ☆☆☆☆☆

#50. Title:

Author: ....

Publisher: ....

Fiction: ○　　　　　　Non-Fiction: ○

Genre / Subject: ....

My review:

....
....
....
....
....
....
....
....
....
....
....
....

Star Rating: ☆☆☆☆☆

Ideas

Ideas for books that I'd love to write:

....

....

....

....

....

....

....

....

....

....

....

....

....

....

....

....

....

....

"When I want to read a novel, I write one."
-Benjamin Disraeli

Ideas

Ideas for books that I'd love to write:

....

....

....

....

....

....

....

....

....

....

....

....

....

....

....

....

....

....

....

....

"I kept always two books in my pocket, one to read, one to write in."
-Robert Louis Stevenson

Ideas

Ideas for books that I'd love to write:

....

....

....

....

....

....

....

....

....

....

....

....

....

....

....

....

....

....

About the Author

SL Beaumont was born and raised in beautiful New Zealand. Her award winning series, *The Carlswick Mysteries,* is available from all good online bookstores. She graduated from the University of Otago, and has worked as a chartered accountant in Auckland, London and New York. When she's not writing, she loves to read and travel.

Printed in Great Britain
by Amazon